ROYALS

WAVE BOOKS SEATTLE & NEW YORK

CEDAR SIGO

Published by Wave Books

www.wavepoetry.com

Wave Books titles are distributed to the trade by

Consortium Book Sales and Distribution

Phone: 800-283-3572 / SAN 631-760X

Library of Congress Cataloging-in-Publication Data

Names: Sigo, Cedar, author.

Title: Royals / Cedar Sigo.

Description: First edition. | Seattle ; New York : Wave Books, [2017]

Identifiers: LCCN 2016049322| ISBN 9781940696522 (limited edition hardcover) | ISBN 9781940696539 (trade pbk.)

Classification: LCC PS3619.I473 A6 2017 | DDC 811/.6–dc23

LC record available at https://lccn.loc.gov/2016049322

Designed and composed by Quemadura

Printed in the United States of America

9 8 7 6 5 4 3 2 1

First Edition

Wave Books 065

FOR BRIAN

—WITH WHOM ALL LANDSCAPES

BECOME LOVE POEMS—

ROYALS

Green Rainbow Song

Hung up on
my hearing
and deep in whose
playbook
one too many
nights and never
a blackout
Doing the best
I can, only a man
it hurts me too
Blues in the Night
Verlaine Blues
sitting here thinking
a blues for Anne
(all nerves)
and mine
the most dirty
unhurried
afternoon jags
A freshly penned
lyric for sinking
to autumnal
Atlantean shade
I wish us more luck
I wish my little
tiger lily sheltered

in a clear crystal
box (being carried)
Green pearl-handled
mallets edging
the annunciation
toward a new burn
The chamber of maiden
thought is metered
Big fields
villagers, stars
on the back-lot blues
It's the smoke spot
I shade softest
a curve so tight
it's really blind
The chamber gives
way to the word
in this case (mine)

Tomorrow Night

Peter's mind is branded
outlandish genius
an emollient golden gas

that shrooms to save its life

O high wasted demons
in legion
crawling in tonight from
over the hill wires aglow
round the stem of a rose
full-on lifted
from the jizz
meth hymnal lines taken home
retooled
for future

autoharp outfits In storm blue
ribbon felled
net of flies

I get the words in shape
to hold out in front

to wail away on those bridges
and the dulcimer kicked

down the stair
unawares   was underwriting
everything
the numbers
and the fix
that little spot
Algeria
on Sunset
. . . nothingness
I got us locked in
and was sort of asked
to leave
Nicely hammered   very true
I stayed in my suit

and stood in the street
silent as a star fallen
dead of exposure

Suspended Sentence

Have we addressed my Scottish
accent in the middle of Baltimore?
That's nicely played
fast-forward to the flashback
that wad of cash
drawn right on the stencil
genuine teenage
lust plus Peter
Hujar the poem floats past
us while I feign bitterness
and weight. Have you not heard
of induction? Forging
new values with the public
who seem to know it's all love
and not theory, all actual
withdrawal of soldiers' bodies
and I, the song (a brise marine)
You'll see the earth smoke
I'll make
no noise
I'm a poet living
upstate
and working as a barber
I rework old railway songs
in a crooked nook
sweeping together

sworn paths
I drink Patrón
for the prettiest little
morning-after bottles
pencil in the track money
memorized per month
containment handed down
in part
from my betters
and mainly well
my old man

Sensation

for Anselm Hollo

Helsinki in good order

in my mind, construction streamlined

separate luminous slivers
tailored toward
the lived in
(to die for)
turning everyone on
at such length
I hung around
and set in mainly
reliving the party
I stepped down
on carved headboards
and on the tapestries
video arcades
became ceilinged
walkways
The dream machines
deal in translation,

Take out "North"

put BLANK
. . . haunting horror . . . escape

Float the next
Etruscan gold split
part of the sky
I like. The ants are red
and black in one body
They carry and lock off

the garnets as seeming
gifts to us

On Strings of Blue

for Bill Berkson

Was it tonight's
flirtatious
remark or his
exquisite songbook
onstage?
My outside life
has turned itself in,
any opening
up at all
is no small feat
when romancing
the edge
of an echo
Smoke in the
dream and rest
in bed,
For all we
know
and I'll
be seeing you,
Carnegie Hall
underground,
"More light, please"
Bill Berkson

will read from
John Wieners
in my wooden
house across
the street (brown
with golden couch)
his sounding out
The Cut, "Not a woman
past, unloved, not
one eye filled
was addressed."
His voice held
the cleanest
copy one
could find,
We scraped
syllables off
the same records,
It's that old
feeling and
I've got it bad,
straight starlight
embarrassing
the big (night)
sky, cool air
unveiled by Bill

Thrones

For Phillis Wheatley: A book of verse uncovered in cornerstones of a Moorish castle, purple and gold, depicting souls in various stages of release, the pitch, anger and arc of the poems an unrhymed mirror to the long Atlantic.

For Jayne Cortez: An intertribal grand entry of poets in cedar bark jackets, split skirts and whalebones pinning them closed, a voice in praise and suspension of the drum.

For Amiri Baraka: The Pisan Cantos decoder ring dipped in black hills gold slipped onto the finger of Donyale Luna who is Cleopatra reborn sleeping soundly in bed.

For Bob Kaufman: A clamp for the mind, docking in a Persian house of ill repute, a striped gabardine diary and the American prison system picked open with an amethyst knife.

For Henry Dumas: A window open on the fog of New York, a studio with desk lamp and a shadow of his writing self pointing back at certain habits, taking off his coat to sit, spilling a little coffee, with all of eternity waiting enthralled.

For Bob Thompson: An all expense paid trip back to Rome on a riverboat tied with roses, its ballroom filled with golden ghouls and hugely debutant postures collapsed, the walls are wet with organ music.

For Alice Coltrane: A custom isolation booth the exact size of Stravinsky's last silhouette, he stares out, he taps from behind the green glass.

For Stephen Jonas: Your favorite Eric Dolphy faded to a room of golden tasseled light, a couch of friends' faces smeared in a gleaming silver crown.

Gauntlet

Twin mystics
(brothers)
about to head farther
underground
to get sucked
off in assignation
tuning my string
to Kitty Wells
clavichord vibrato
feathered tall
as the Superdome
in full-blown
fez capped furor
destruction
of any poetic
art impossible
traction's ingrained
even in abandon
scrawled black
ghost dance
rehearsal
lightning eyes
exceptional
containment
strike a second
print in service

to the waxen moon
blood drops
larger than vials
we scraped the
sea monsters off
the maps and
proceeded to
the boiler
only his words
were saved from
the paintings
writing through
a ledger, black
and white entwined
to heal I guess
it works. Egyptian
quick draw dotted
stains with static
fell out of bed
for a hundred
a week, poets
are the finest
undervalued
jewelers, urchins
of mascara smeared
trunk songs
tapped slowly
into my skull

After the Oracle

First
time in a long time
the depth of impression
is straight ahead
overall condition noted
continued
Change
the angle of approach
the beam always widens
and lightsabers
surround the doorways
to save us
I'm turning the poem
around in my window
for joy
and there is
no text
begging to drop by
allowing for such a thing
so hot
that setting sun,
rocks held by taut strings
The silk
of furniture
is burned alive
by a Futurist

a linoleum cut of a gash
clean the spit valve
(not often)
Kit caught his bus
Emeryville
before a train to Portland to read
tell them all hi
I cut the small
black shadow
of a jet and
am moving it about
the sky
in the postcard
Mount Olympus (blue)
Bailey Range
from Hurricane Ridge
right here with you
after all
night

7-20-14

The Vision

My typewriters to be melted and cast

as a bell. Twin water snakes strangled

by their capes

waiting to go off on prepared piano, a round of French

to float my bits of hugely failed Paul Verlaine Blues,

the hat blocked

and golden rising lines. A pop song scrawled

beneath the water stained wall,

I found it impossible

not to dwell in the words, reading billboards

between the strip. I left on the bit about relaxing

enough to get the drift and hand it back erect, in stitches.

Bleach in the flash

imprinted on the iris, emblazoned crown

in full dissolve.

To melt your barroom portrait or perfectly toned bust

tilted into bronze

beside the assassin ridden balconies

((vacuum mounted surround sound assassins))

Bombing through any era's

open inquisition, we were fathomless and beating the clock,

all night within reach.

The iron maiden, nose guarded helmets in line

riding the most haunted wave and mirror

grown over with stars.

Medallion

for Michael McClure

How well I know that
flowing spring in black
of night
Alone and chosen
left to form
this one-off
wilted dispatch
written for the feast
long held
in our room
below language
Color forms a pantomime
for the maze
descent in green
A syndicate
is stranded
face-out
all stars
all charges
to unfold out from torment
to recognition
A spiral cut to the headlands
reading as ancient

no future
The door swung
till the roots ripped
waiting on the drift
and blindingly
restored works
man himself
a light
The sheet is lifted
on voices
those securing their fix
O hanging them back
on doors that groan
how swept apart
too soon

* *

The higher
he ascends
the darker the wood

The grain in the line
senses addition

emerging at
once as
it all begins

to end, all lies
shot back
to the start

the most elusive
shot frozen, bloodied
one of one

* *

On that happy night
in secret, no one saw
me through the dark
A light projection/pink moon
on black barn door
a jar of light
grown large
behind three slats
plastic overlay of words
a fluid mine
no camera
meaning obstruction
Stained cardboard
on strings
slide the doors
to be oblivious
to joining
in music
pulling open the mirrors
to dark bars

where I could see down
upon a man's skull
I built my own circuitry/sounds
and flow insisted
upon my own armory
a hall of humans
those poets
I stop to remember
in flooded motion

Like Stride

We will live forever misaligning the changes
into further time stinted tricks
giving up post kickflip failures
scribbling prepared remarks to notebooks
unlocked over dry spells flooded with demand
salt crystals crushed, the past flashed
and I was a working writer, nursing the pools
in everyone's hearts, disembarking
soothing the air around a final question
away in the country toweling off
my doing the most proper thing turned
somehow slick, of feminine wiles, a clap trap
case book, the dream at the end so delicate
and put out. Makes light so pained
two reclining long in the turn of the neck
in like stride, imparting poetic asides
(bored to tears in Taos) cross out words
and tunnel the line, the guts will sit atop
glistening, hand stamped valves really
toying with release, a lighted display
corresponding controls, to repave
an entire arcade in release of our well
whiskey texting back dimension
We are poor and not cheap, in love
with the same little song slashed booklet

Whims

I drew a French mustache
onto a John Cage postcard

I dreamt a circular squirting flower
onto Morton Feldman's lapel

I strung a torn taffeta gown
up and down John Wieners

I handcrafted a Rolex
onto the wrist of Rene Ricard

I spun a haunted pendant
for the edges of Anne Waldman

I stamped and numbered an opium pipe
for Gregory Corso's private room

I handwrote a Ouija board
for CAConrad and set it outside the door

The sun came up wet and bright red
I carved a two-man canoe for Brian and myself

Ode for Nine Voices

Earth seems the haloed side of a flat stone

flaunting its gold-blooded diamondback secrets
That we are all one,
that we haven't the privilege or time to change our minds

I chance on a lyre to liven the lights
to bear down
up my coast
on rims
to roll out . . .

The mirror and corridor both have voices,
they are without attendant siren
I was a Bolinas separatist poet
where the epigrams say more
when cannibalized
Held aloft in a fog of queer voicings
when the waves are altered to approximate
the kiss
and death
and haunting

in the woods behind the house. We shall restage
Apollinaire's last hot march into evening air
Excuse my fragile spiral,

excuse my horse cock unveiled in Byzantium
No longer alone in the hotel-casino made famous by poetry
lashing every mixed feeling on black against the walls
the most incisive jagged script for twelve hands
one is trapped in vocoder delay and dates horribly

The first spasm
blanks in the guns of the trees
each line peeled and bitten, brushed out from its paper
The poets in glowing lab coats
expository prose, lightning white arms crossed with strobes
I turn my spade to the inset language

turning up late every other night
to demonstrate my own take on the sonnets, the lyric
even the most dividing
arrested arts of love

Mornings in Mexico

for Brian Marr

Admire tiny coiled pots

Make cave paintings
on postcards for Mom

All saints

Are freed from their hollows

Clean the pipes
and small onyx

Mirror-early reflections

Rent *A Place in the Sun*

Hire a car

Listen to *Girls*

Vomit
Watch the video

Buy water

Pass endless rows of totems
(Abalone eyes)

Count boats on the moonlight
(CLOSED)

Strip-tease for the sauna maid

The gay guide is free
and imprisons me

Buy a black painted ram's head (shellacked)

Wear it around

Shop well together

Guns of the Trees

A set of notes detailing the caves of an impeccable gentleman, a minotaur poet. The most devastating silence of the first ten books. A fantasy of Philip Lamantia as an action figure stripped naked with special audible scream switch buttons. Reimagining Grace Cathedral as the great symphonic hall of coconuts, O the book is resting complete in a Chinatown basement.

A poem I puked drying out at a hot springs in love winding through the dry hills of neem leaves, an exaggeration of music I thought younger poets admired. The trimmings I knew I could press new meaning in between. I was endlessly in the mood and working this lace front, that words as force walk the earth. I tried to show a sailor bounding through his life in silhouette.

I'd rather live on my own with my magic lantern. I'm sick of public schools that reek of church. Drink. Fuck. Breed. Light the top shelf. Pressed green woods with light standing even straighter. He is standing on my eyelids and his hair is crossed with mine. Giving flat girders to the dream poem. It's all about the filthy paint of a room that empties out at night. Scotch tape wrapped words

guarding fissures of light. Brakhage and Bob Dylan jokes I wrote exclusively for money for The Recluse. Fished out from the threshing odds and ends. A song I thought was lost, the lines were nothing on their own. A diorama whose language goes ahead to shatter the glass. Billion dollar kickflips in your honor.

A perfect approximation of the opening smile. His poetry would make great bronzed Inuit blues. My feast was in the easy blood that flowed. A dark skittering travelogue I almost didn't type up, the most break up like drivel. Number thirty-five with lines from two sonnet cycles. Translations via telephone, such civil war is in my love and hate. Lines in which I know the way

the music lays. I back away from the wall. I wanted the deepest impression, a line torn from its plush root. Occupy damaged or inspired, they are reverse black Nazis in unfunded wheelchairs. I can't keep up. Wiping black snot onto white sleeves. Another last ditch genius fuck. The morning after a long night hot in Fort Greene. Back on the West Coast writing it. Desk faces wall. A Chinese distillation to

illustrate the offing, panels for the walls of heaven really concealing its canals, haranguing the Provençal into a blues again. It closes too tightly. Trample it down to its esteemed place in language arts. In homage to his wealth, and willingness to go down on his masters. A matter of course under Bismarck bridges. It's more a leaving off of the grime sometimes, entered cities of boiling red dust.

Photographing Theatre

Underpass drowned
in moonlight
the tunnel
allows the wood
and ghost of
a young girl
her expression
so vanished
carries us

Cosmos in
the joining
of three tiles
an angel
touches
her breasts
sharp stylus
left alone
two ballroom
ladies
crosshairs
at each
of their hearts

Older Zuni
woman

hair tied
back in a bun
shoulders tight
and high
and never to turn
the hyper blond
child is twisted
caught
looking back

Family
pictures dead
queens
white flares at
the top
in points on
black
a stark winter
tree
smiling skeletons
light drawn in
at their temples

The spider
was
a loosely
constructed
coral choker
the legs went
on forever

cut in two
hairs one
up and
one down

Lisbon first
night and
early morning
"Is it ok
for you to
play alone
barely
hidden from
the street? It's
ok we
pull the furniture
outside here
to sit."

Smear
of dried
flowers school
pictures the
stems on
the roses and
spattered
paper left at
the desk
a mind haunted
by its screen

Two brothers
guard a sleeping
child smaller
his spirit swiped
down mother bent
to kiss him
the second frame
all the same
rushed in
wallpaper
and posters tacked
under wet paint

Crowded underworld
some are in
pure unaggravated
sleep
men fully dressed
heads thrown back
seated
hands folded

You could
see her
ripped from
his side
at the cold
bus station
a broad
single slash

at the screen
gone forever

A Polish
woman scarf
tied at the
chin steel
eyes carrying
alchemical
pipe pointed
heavier
at one end
her kneeling
sister with basket
beside her
sticks slipping from
the pile legs
fogged at the
knee and torn

A reclining
boy model
an old
Victorian
smears
to move
the lawn down
into the sky

Roses playing
telephone the
bodice wants up
and in along
the bottom
more of a designer
than poet or
painter moviemaker
the strain
behind the image
starts over

Fever Dream

Three Inuit boys flirt across the fire
It is set snugly centered in the glacier
A rainbow is erected from hammered bands of steel
Bearing the color of sunburned breasts
The boys take turns tacking them up
Until the tacks burst out from the wall
They hang it all again not facing me
It's getting hot with the rainbow finally up and running
The boys rid themselves of their parkas and climb through
A human head sized hole, oiled with the inside fat of a black moose
Shining in pink and unspooled crowns of blue, an outline
They each crawl into and emerge riverside on steep snowy banks
Perfect cooling currents move in line
The boys return to the hole, stand around
Laughing and reheat themselves

The Magic Mountain

I dreamt I was an orator
trapped in a typewriter–

Now I seem to have
come out on
the other side:

My mind seizes on
the form first

(There
is
no
free
verse)

I color in
the outline as one would
the border of a country

whatever techniques
are called upon

to welcome the body
of the poem

into the room

Incision

for Norma Cole

The gauze

in hair-sprayed lilac

mist
out from her green box

she draws
innumerable
diagonal swords

each pointed
inward
definite kingdoms
announcing their
grip in flickers
always with adjacent
alloyed
countinghouse a blizzard

of crystal is blushing
outside the searchlights

all shored up
at rest
full pleasure
past our secret

We will continue in our work
and bodies
no choice
as to when
architecture
must intervene
(sun beheaded—blank—no blood)

It is the occasional
bend in a turnpike
a long curve
to break

my fitful sleep
A trampling heard
clearly
intermittent
nails
pounded around
the door
more snow
is springing loose

Our Lives

for Julian Talamantez Brolaski

Thinking back
after all
we have done
just to write
it plainly as fact
would be beautiful

with no choice
tangle
or conveyor
for rest
words get
replayed endlessly
anyway

our light
shall be termed
queer
and superior
STAR

Blue Moon

after Alfred Starr Hamilton

(1)

For I pulled my blue coat over my subway sleeve
I had to leave to let the cat out
I had just enough change to ride it to the end
The lines corresponded to the rainbow bolted map
I was nearly shot, the same vampires casting about underground
The country folk had caught up with my manner of hearing
Such resonant shapes meant danger
(The golden poem is a flower dropped on its head
Broken open, bleeding in a pool)
And through death we incite further poets
We nail the old bottles to the wooden box

*

Aren't we all dying to vacation?
Aren't we all mad from wasted money?
Aren't we all scribbling into invisible lockets?
Aren't we all trying to form the perfect search?
Don't we wish to be left alone in a workroom?
Aren't we all waiting for the cake to cool until it's iced?

*

A brown rooming house withered
Kept up all night
With frozen flickering lights

(2)

Sometimes I think
I write aloud–
lift encased amulets
to the old wall
Trust their radiance
will breathe forth
then fume–the blood
puddles–runs slick
leaves stuck on grass
tips–text quivers
with the ghost of
a pink tongue cut
–mimic so closely
as to poison the line
let the machine thrash
about to bloody us
for industry–its shining
pick under lights–lace
cut mats–I was thinking
solely of the wet
blue chrysalis outing
itself–a prime cut
of steam advances
drawing on

fissures of the old
earth to float
our map—the
unimproved
future tense

(3)

The sky is slow to be tricked tonight

chamber blues
are freezing violet
his silhouette crowned

felt long in the tooth
as deeply etched
as powdered a likeness
of Alfred Starr Hamilton

himself a writer and tinker, antennae

Moonlight falls
as a gown
down through the black
cage
an empty tree

Demand a larger cage, offstage
of sound and darker woods
a mean shine
Be a sweetheart,
a weatherman

be the disobedient
wavering hem
or command the words
to hang back
to tip their hat
and live alone
Send several masterpieces (poems)
several times a day
lying

bright
in the same
cold box

A Passage

The dream
closet is no longer
cordoned off.
It vanishes easily (the active phrase assumes direction).
Happy as a brain-dead heiress,
the entourage involved forever turning its back,
unveiling of arrival,
glimmering beyond a list of books that have disappeared.
Felix of the Silent Forest is still missing.
It is one long wait for the elevator,
my empty mind faces a mirror.
No objects but audible words formed Death Metal,
Solid Gold, and Country Blues.
The camera turns unannounced,
another misfit that would recognize my eyes.
Mascara marbled sweat,
beyond frightened
only fierce.
Uninterested
in stories
only how they're held.
Calling up receptors of individual visions,
clear to the center of the gallery.
Pleasing perfect strangers,
songs to lift our spirit into tanzanite teacups.
Take a walk outside,

a chance meeting as he demanded
and argued his way through a letter.
That I was a double of my self
and owed him money on top of his outrage.
I sported a glow in the dark mustache
to throw him off
to lock the door behind me,
alone against my charts and untrained voices.
I read poetry as if from coloring books or paint
with water,
joining the raised golden dots.
I must have slept with no way of getting in touch.
I woke up to my lover then
breaking down the door.

The Wigwam

I join each frame by hand and smooth them myself
Some mornings I have to stop short, if I can't run a comb
through my hair I'm no good to anyone (except for the poets)
Dipping into plans for clear portals, a breath between worlds
I will only know revolution in real life where plans laid are still kept
A big reveal in store as I shift the reading onto legs,
drop my collarbone out front. It's a long-range barrel
particular to hours of tinkering. My morning shed is kept warm
despite when having left. I can draw a cloth over its roof
with the inside pulley. The fog turns to white faking jade determinants,
blown clouds, a fat razor wet on its side forms a helmet
in its filthy, stealth manner of light, contented to carve onto
whose dressing screen? Soon junked, later resurfaced as
a delicate carriage house of an uncollected

A Handbook of Poetic Forms

I use acrostics to get laid
Then pulp to pay my rent
And ballads to buy off the Christians
Sonnets to learn counterfeit
Chant to reverse dark circles
Cantos trigger insanity and worse
Terza rima when I feel like swimming laps
Odes for luck in blackjack
Index for sedative
A prayer to form searchlights
Haiku to throw a shadow and tear it in half
A diary to become more gay
Pantoums to pace the cave paintings
Limerick to lock a private room
Blues to light my face in a fedora
Rap to have my postures blown out
Lyric to form my shaving mirror
Sestinas to map my double life

Panavision

for Sarah Enid Hagey

I miss you, shivering
on air, a star
moving me through New York

I see the leaves dangle
through a crack in the door
through light
I am a stylist of lines of
stems in release

slow and broken
spray of bullets

beyond the use of sound
to lift a square
          stone god

We have completely
run out
of Egyptian slaves

No lapse in poise
walking onto the happy set
of *A Fatal Desire*, *The Godmother*,
or *Lovelorn Domestic*

Boys meet Sarah

Sarah meet the boys

Legs crossed in makeup
bright and early
a bank of midnight blue
onyx backing you up

Poems for Saints

(1)

Who raised his dream forest
who managed to hand the cross
to the poet
just before the film burnt up
or the money ran out

(2)

Thrown
As a palm
Of breath
That is found
To be
A mirror

(3)

I would pluck
a strand, a wire
to paint your silhouette
in blazes
on a snuffbox

(4)

She was never scared straight
she was a pair of ladies' voices combing the cave

(5)

Bury my shoes
Gone to blood-red brown
Hanging down
Thirsty for fire

(6)

Farther on
starlight trembles
over the thought
of the act

East River strings
turnabout
in a green toned night

(7)

Her greatest works
were fired in gold

A stairway
with a single light
all
the way
up

(8)

Thin
strands
of
music
spike
to
override
all
life
outside

(9)

To boil the marsh tea
Eat carnation mush

Steam a rack of wool
To bend the wooden box

Satin Glass

for Julien Poirier

Set desire
Is a long drip
A knocked out
Quarry
American
Constantine

Smokeless
Powders
Bolt + Star
A grate
In mint green
Copper pins
Suspended palace
Of lovers
Rejoined
Of gliding by
In boredom
Unbecoming
Huge door
In the wall
Too smart Phoned in
Not dead enough
Swig

Of the yellow
Eye pressed
Electric organ
I asked
Men who did
Flower the lights
Violet in lime
On gray
Noises
I remember were
Minerals forming
Their one mountain
Tears that quivered
In rage
Pulling into flames

The Real Contents of a Street Poet's Suitcase

Tiny dented copper spools
An elephant gun
Clean underwear
Red Garland records (*Red in Bluesville*, *Red Alone*)
A pair of counterfeit Vachel Lindsay cuckoo clocks
Empty pocket rocket (Fernet)
Cerulean rabbit's foot keychain
Turquoise money clip
Seventeen cents
Stained satin pajamas
Golden Sardine (with underlined lines and figures)
"Apollinaire never hiked in papier-mâché woods"
"Apollinaire never slept all night in an icehouse"

Side Trips

I saw
at my desk nightly
using only
streetlight . . .
I blow-dry the basement tape for Jack to read
my drunken crash at the gates
—endless cartoon color-blind blues—

the ghost of John Jacob Niles is flown
to what graven rock, shaking
in his boots, he melts the ravine
drinks up the river
a sun wasted rose color
"It
was only
a baggage room
and attic, here
where we lived before the war
that first broken window over
It shocked me with the levels
of felicity and of
imagination
inside"

twin angels
at the impasse

stripping wire
out from
the earth

bolts of thunder pealed
from under the
falls

stones
thrown (from very high)
to form
a ziggurat
an hourglass
I almost forgot
to intone
The blood in the iron
bowl/old warehouse torched
on a quiet night,
"formulas opening the
floodgates"
meaning my Ode to Martha Diamond
meaning a blank book for Lucy Rose classic
tiny
split-second poems
that clung to the air
beneath my gaze

Watching William Castle Writing

He pokes in and out of several privately printed editions, often rereading aloud passages we first thought riddled with chance. It's the total possession that takes hold as he moves toward the notebook that becomes a deep secret. Not so much his wrought iron slips in the line or the several attached vanished voices. What makes it down onto the screen as letters, words, phrasing, seems after the fact. It is this desire to filter the language that we have captured continuously. Most of our men propped up in the rafters with the various wires are signaling the switch Off and On. He will often sing the glimmering hook of a line and let it lead him to music halls, to gilded backstage dressing mirrors. He bends at the waist to melt a voice in pitch black, a discourse on method. His phone calls never betray any new angles. If anything he repeats himself so you are forced to listen to events of the past few days with waning enthusiasm. He never speaks of all the anonymous lovers. It doesn't seem to matter. He will either write it out as pulp or make drawings. The line is just as overwrought either way and gets it twisted. His clinical claim on madness may secure an objectivity. Most readers will claim an immediate distance from this element. He draws storyboards for the threads he hasn't the guts to write. That one in which the young editor is finally admitted by the widow to read the last manuscript, rumored incomplete. The editor has several desperate poets lined up for the filling in. Poets can be best at simply matching tones of voice. The dead writer had the guts to start first and that sets them at ease. They drop by the press in person like beasts for their checks, chattering like royals and bathed in relief. Telling all the best jokes looser than their poems.

Setting Out Late

for Jackson Meazle

The skyline and the sea blur
into smooth solid squares

I set out late
for downtown, a clutch of lights
that misfire, shaken

in the distance
Blowing all the bills
I set aside because
he tells me to . . . . . .

My gift poems this year
were impossible:

A mournful, Germanic
Orange Blossom Special

A silent film star
I hired to climb the walls and to
sulk in your bed

A silkscreen of a 1975 sunrise

Soundscapes for five separate cigarettes

There are no stairways,
no *Sing Out* reel to reels

Only blue grass and brushfire
racing the hills
your one night only rendition of
Two for the Road

Moon River wider than
my first poem/painting
pulled from the caves

Writing all my life toward
one stone print

2 RED HANDS

Portrait in Black

Love is a trance anyway . . .
poised Egyptian queen of the compound accent.
The moon is down in the offstage dark
and the demons in tears,

long dead, half under the shade. They lie facedown in the long passage.
I go full-on spaz,
(all asides)
imperfect pitch.
A sutra for hobbling harpsichord—
cobwebbed keys
thinner than reeds.

The amp would cut out at key points
in line with my little suede two step.
The service I provide is a more addictive series,
worn plots are left deep,
hung queens get hanged for the warm red crush.
We have to talk in every room to solve the dream house,

to consider which poems I will allow to be lyred and felt up,
perused over shots, blunts in a
smoke stained study. My heart is the most fucked country,
a sketched, uneven valley grove of bones.
You can only capture the poets
and keep them lurking . . .

When everyone seems an undercover
statuette of eruptions.
The lady caps her brandy
in wretched
unmistakable silence.

Smoke Flowers

I stayed shut up in my room
A red wooden table took up most of it (and tools)
A black unlined journal filled my days
The dark of the woods breathing in through the window
My dad's friends and all of their kids asleep everywhere our house would hold them

I moved to my mother's for good at fourteen
I soon left school for dreams of the lyric (of building)
I lied and said the lessons moved too slowly
Caught the ferry back to Seattle
Dragging back my bags of books . . . Allen, Jack, John Wieners

I filled in a few blues songs to form a whole story
Couldn't carry it. Marveled at the graveled voice of the devil
Sounded good, on pitch, rich, illiterate. Moved away to study
Stretched what little money there was (did not work)
I was mostly taught who to read . . . Robert Duncan, Creeley, Joanne

Burned out on college my third year, suddenly it seemed the Golden Fleece
When I only needed sex. I was driven across country in the manner of a dark prince
Still couldn't write well, only trying. The filters on the words felt waterlogged and stuck

Flew out to San Francisco, penniless. Left a woman crying facedown in the Chelsea
Pulled myself up and lived a year with my bathroom down the hall. No buzzer
Moved down with the sun to a new life, found work. The long leaning tower of nights
Fell to mesh. I became a warrior surprised at what I still didn't know, how to get started,
Move along, stay moving, how to fill the page all over.

Three Landscapes

(L.A. Odyssey)

I almost insist on the words
as doors left swinging

from the force no one saw.

A wrap around hotel

with empty courtyard

boarded up, sprayed white

Hiding Out.

Nick is too kind,
two black
and slowly moving marbles against flesh.

Sara, a model of containment,

Brian is luminous (all eyes)

twin fires beyond the pit
that only crackles green

brighter than the edges of neon
lining Fairfax:

Family Books

The Films of Robert Blake

We score a trim ocean

blue

windbreaker

and *Dinosaurs of the Land, Sea and Air*

I slipped away from the bench
when they brought
the car around.

My black hobo sack abandoned

and thought a bomb. I was seamlessly high on my air heels and driven

away
to where the camera could not follow.

(Tyler, Texas)

Two out-of-towners
in the sharp grasses
white churches
not a hair feels out of place
They say the next county over
from Smith is wet.

You go around Ben Wheeler
Through dumb-fuck Whitehouse
Back over Black Beauty Ravine

Drink till mothers due
back at the home (for memory care)
and a random viewing of *East Side, West Side*.
(Where Stanwyck and Ava Gardner step into the same picture)

Finally alone together,
more arrowhead hunting.
We are fuses left scorched under lavender skies–
where Karen Carpenter's longest note
is broken in half.

Near dark
I shot what I thought
was a long stick
and didn't check back for two days.
It was a water moccasin

head all blown off
and caved in
slick as snot.

(in memory of David Langston)

(In and around Port Angeles)

Crescent was the lake

and Aircrest

a motel

mind stuck at my sources

A flimsy strip
of rooms
painted,
spotless insides

A blossom curled to its drink
in the glass jar

fluid as past saviors and poet
explorers

Philip

With the shade
of Miss Kids

"Any rough land rises with light"

A peeling red house
rotten wood trim

It felt empty from across the river
I was a giant
bent at the waist
with massive reach

(through lines of rain)

combing knots from the fog

clear down
through the pine

Tiny points
of bloody
lime ink rejoined

every image
meaning light pressed
the day long . . .

menacing chord–

congested
hall of mosses

bump
and narrow bridge

I fell out alone and

so solid

reciting my crystalline
little head off
in slick
and banded verse

"O the air

from the valve

that burns

which glyph"

Aquarelle

after Emile Nolde

Bent at my
desk
in pieces
in starlight's
wire clutch
the eye is caught
staring into splinters
like the warble of
the dove at the start
of rain, and the curve
of the cane
to follow its script,
the Lord of
the Nadir is
the black sun,
a hot whiskey
with anise wash,
small circular brush
to lash and gather
to be trans
not destroyers
continuous snowfall
recorded, crystals
tapping colors

out from their centers
my idealized
voice in fact
a ruin
I can't freeze
lines together
any longer
I need hot flowers,
figures ripped
loudly from
their boxes rather
off balance
crumbling smoke
losing the light
lifted

Crescent

(1)

I stand empty
beside the armor
shadows flinch
They close
around us
I stand back
and blink—reappear
farther back
I break into a sweat
It glows and I wave
back to my dead

(2)

We natives are royals
Yet phantoms
The edges emblazoned, clear
From fingertip to foot
Seattle is empty and surrounded
The sun beheaded or
Am I a marked man?
I will sing to skin the shadows
Till they feel worn

And pointed (rocking)
Bothered by the wind
A new measure is blown open
Threatening–threading the room.
I listen (painfully close)
Beyond the heightened fear
Of recapture
I take a long cold shower
Before I dress . . . . . .
I sing the diamond to my crown
Creep farther out of town
A tangle of fog and bloodied
Dust motes landed
Loud laughter in the dark

(3)

I thought back on my birthday
our wandering downtown together

the strings were in tune
played and passed
like a maiden into heaven

Elevators work their way up the sky
a jet thrashed in lightning
Hello, Nice to see you,
I have no light,
whiskey neat in my glass

The man at the bar is set and straight (no question)
It's a filthy night under the bare bulbs

my whole body
jerks left
right

(4)

I teach occasional
overnight
courses
Kickball with Demons,
Jet Set Contours and
Comprehension,
How to Stalk the Police
down your own Streets
or speaking on exactly
how my voice
got to sound
so shot
so high
how the goddess
retreads nightly
with all
approach notes
and neighboring
slack
pricked of

the torture & crystal
gardens
wherein I dreamt I could drive
and I did
figure eights
the light streamed
opposite
orange gases
swarming off both
sides
I kept
an eye out
for Indians also
(always) first trace
of sunrise
three
planks
crosscut red
key missing
the left
hand stumbles
close to home, stuck
& strained to
wander
in the tip
and bite of the light
I staple in
more smoke
and a bit
later on

illusion
a torn
& bloodied crest
oh and bodies
floated up
near the corners
overnight
It was never
words themselves
but the instant
they took up
as marked
as reset

(5)

Pure black
steeple
steadier than
my blade
man
in robes
mushroom shrinks
hands are
clasped
the middle
part
of a ribbon
snake

flashed
rabbits foot
necklace
tiny gun
& baron's crest
Tahitian dancer
in mid-wave
doll
frozen there
seal of
the Templar
hand
held out
to beckon
beyond
the lock
in the screen
a bag
of bones
leaning
stabs
the flag
onto
stolen islands
archbishops
garden of
headgear
white where
black should be
silver

      Buddha
steam leaving
           in a huff
       from behind
his head
jet
    in a nosedive
so close up
          my phone
bleeds harder
          than a brick—
        broken cross

(6)

A carriage cuts
through Red River Valley
down Vail's gate
round Highland
Falls

much of my time
is taken up
on the way
to various readings
hours spent
holding my gun
and set
list delirious

I need not shoot
till it's sundown
and pointed
language trapped
at well worn angles
need not be read
aloud
to cut away from
to add a two lane
bridge
or patch of fire

We pick out which
of the lines are hooks
steer clear
of all else
keep the one
foot nailed and
fucking up
the stone floor

slashing verse
in nail-polish
out of boredom
or near bankruptcy
It's all cleared up later
as you are found
starving, still
handsome
a body stuck

behind the
living room
door

(7)

We are shrinking stars
in relation to the altar
Push your hand
through the holes
a giant violet bank of clouds
The edge on the moon speaks
all the way around

ACKNOWLEDGMENTS: Some of these poems have appeared in: *Poem-a-Day*, *The Emerald Tablet*, *STEDT*, *"T" Book* Vol. 4, *The Wave Papers*, *MARY: A Journal of New Writing*, *OmniVerse*, *Amerarcana*, *Cordite Poetry Review*, *Mud City Journal*, *Bronze Chimes: Poems after Alfred Starr Hamilton*, *Dream Closet*, *OAR*, *Asterisk*, *Elderly*, *Helix Syntax*, *Poetry Now*, *Poems for John*, *Breather #1*, *LXAQ*, *The Volta*, Broken Broadsides by Expedition Press, *SWP DIY Guerilla Mag 2016*, Pacifica Broadside Series, *Selected Works of Cedar Sigo and Frank Haines*, *NUMBER 2*, *Foglifter*, *Nepantla: A Journal Dedicated to Queer Poets of Color*, and Low Res Broadside Series.

The author wishes to thank: All of my editors at Wave Books, Ryo Yamaguchi, Brian Marr, Oscar Tuazon, Frank Haines, Colter Jacobsen, Joanne Kyger, Donald Guravich, Peter Burghardt, Anthony McCann, Jennifer Foerster, Norma Cole, Johnny Ray Huston, Julien Poirier, Rod Roland, Nicholas Weist and The Shandaken Project, Alli Warren, Chris Duncan, Joe Ferriso, Casey O'Neal, Anne Waldman, Mark Allen, Elizabeth Orr, Matt Connors, Tenaya Nasser-Frederick, Mary Cisper, Layli Long Soldier, Diane di Prima, and Micah Ballard.